The Way it Was

The Way it Was

Poems by

A.M. Brandt

Cover design by Shay Culligan
Cover photograph by Tom Chambers

ISBN: 978-1-952326-49-3

Kelsay Books
502 South 1040 East, A-119
American Fork, Utah, 84003

Gratitude to the following:

Savannah College of Art and Design, Fine Arts Work Center, and Spoleto Writers' Retreat. Special thanks to Jim Moore and to Darren Morris, whose steadfast good will and wicked smarts have been vital.

For Kenneth & Faye, as always.

Acknowledgments

Potomac Review: "The Way with Students"

Cider Press Review: "Prayer"

National Poetry Review: "For a Luminous Singing"

Parhelion Literary Magazine: "The Future of Anywhere,"
"Impulse Control," "Strawberries," "Ways of Sympathy,"
"The Host"

The Cortland Review: "The Falling"

Cimarron: "Precision" "Lines on Disaster"

The Sewanee Review: "Concerning the Axe," "A Harvest,"
"Elegy to Carelessness," "A Solitary Romance"

The Southern Review: "Driving to Work"

Kalliope: "We Thought We Heard Rain"

Journal of Curriculum Theorizing: "Porcelain Picture in a Hilltop
Cemetery, Spoleto, Italy," "My People"

Contents

Driving to Work

Here comes the old man with his coffee
and brown spaniel who goes crazy with wagging
to find the bus-stop kids in their loose confederacy.
The girl in leg braces wears sweats and a Windbreaker,
holds her mother's hand. It's spring again; the apple
green buds are only blowsy stains against a frail sky.
My own daughter at home in her bed, sick
after a three-day fever. Last night I held her
in the bath, laid her body against mine and dipped
her hair to the running water, her eyes
openly deliberate to this world and the other one
half-hidden. And I thought of that famous photograph
of the mother and child, that nearly grown girl arching back
in a kind of tense spasm, the mother all soft and relaxed
with a love of one who has been allowed to hold
her daughter forever. Children on the radio, too, real children
all over Ireland and the ones in church orphanages
and the thousands of charges, *thousands*
over the years. How will they ever bear
to be touched and held again?
My students are rising and dressing,
traveling by city bus or bike or car.
They will be waiting in the classroom,
for something or anything
to happen in their lives. Tired after nights
of new love or tired of too little love.
I don't know how it is that I can come before them,
hopeful as they are or deserve to be.
I'm trying hard to believe in something as buoyant
as the Bradford Pears along the road, blowing
their white blossoms in a sudden flurry.
They keep doing that. Each year shimmering all at once,
making impossible beauty, then throwing it away.

Undressing Story

When bending to pull off my boots
    I do not see myself in the antique mirror,
and when I reach back for the zipper

I let my dress fall where it lands
    as if I were alone
in my own house.

It happens all the time, what I call
    the unseeing.

I'll be picking up a fork or pulling a cloud of hair
    from the brush, careful to bundle
it all together and I'll be doing it, seeing

myself in the vanity mirror
    above the sink, cut sideways in angle
of shoulder or sunken cheek

but what I see is someone
    unfamiliar as I've always been.

All this dressing and undressing. Brush of space
    we make of ordinary time.
Just like I part my lips the same when
    I put on lipstick, pucker and kiss the tissue.

I am good at this routine unbeing. I wash the dishes
    with care, I drive with easy abandon, but I don't
see my eyes in the rearview mirror, I don't see

my knees, in bed, bent just so every time.
       It hardly mattered for years.
And then I was hurrying the other day, changing

into jeans in front of the long gilt mirror in the bedroom
       and suddenly I could see myself really see
me where I stood; something settled and stilled,

and the longer I stayed, the more I conceded
       to what I'd never and had always been.
As a gradual amassing of gestures

arrange blue eye to animate blue unblinking,
       double lipped, unembarrassed, I
believed nothing had changed until

my daughter called from the hallway and I looked
       away, finished dressing, and stood still,
while the other me went out through the door.

For a Luminous Singing

After the lavender of day is done and I lie
awake in the tomb between your father and me,

I sound your name, one softening syllable,
a sterling resonance to what is left of you

inside of me. Daughter that feels the sacrament
of stones, you say you are sick of being a stone

that falls back, barely moves, tumbles but a little way.
Tonight, you're doing it again, a vagary of wings

that cross over rivers, through groves of alders,
to that place of solace marked away.

You are learning the laws of forgetting
the dark moon that was ours alone.

One shoulder grows damp; the other is a wheat field
burnished for a hard red winter to come.

Creation Myth in Retrograde

In this version of the story
a woman is swimming in a clear

blue pool. Awash in swirls and mirages,
the water eddies along her body

as she moves. She goes under
in the sudden silence.

Her arms, so used to holding,
open wide and return to her with

nothing but the old story. A woman
is swimming in a lake where no one

can save her. The shoreline falls away
behind her. You know this story.

A woman is swimming
in an ocean. Fathoms fall away

beneath her. It is night. She floats
in a planetary reflection

until the twinning of her body
dissolves all the children

of the world in the one
dark dome of her womb.

Sovereignty

On the third, final, and most intimate level, women interacted with male pirates by becoming pirates.

—*Bandits at Sea*

Inside the starboard window
of my room the men know me
by another name. I, alone, unbind
my breasts. It is enough.
It is the promise of brotherhood
and the intricately carved hours
in a freedom I could not fathom.
I am tired, but my mind drifts
amid the sea wrack that gathers
near the map maker's final ledges.
Days at a dangerous horizon line
where birds are fearless.
And when the rough patterns of cliffs
appear, I open my clothes
to no one. I foresaw a boundless love,
the men simple in their need, the crying
and pounding sea. Here, what holds me
are only the jackstays, trunnels, and cordage
of my own unburdened heart.

Things Being What They Are

Here you are, and also here
in the rise and set of a rainy winter.

Here in domestic wherever, the city steaming
in freeze and thaw, the face of the caged

yard rose stretching.
For all the past is present

and ever so. And the body hurts,
rolls over to face profligate dawn.

Ransacked beauty, the intercoastal
emptying out there.

Strange inheritance, the maternal
desire to care for anyone

but myself. Earnest spasm, my own
history forfeited, where my name

and the one or ones unnamed
gather together at the gates of day,

children of iron, sulfur, leaf and thorn,
meager in our eagerness to go forth

and go forth to be freed
to what lesser freedoms afford.

Through Wires

I don't even know
      how a record player works, how the needle lifts
minute vibration from a black shining all the way through last
century,
      or what delivered your voice, say, like a hankie

caught mid-wave over actual telephone wires
      years ago. Now it feeds through synaptic
virtual lightning resembling nothing I know.

Once, I made a communion of nail-punctured cans and string,
      a secret system of listening. I believed
in the magic-ocean held within a glass cupped to a door

where I knelt, straining for the near species-love one
      might note in a moment of effortless
kindness. But it's not enough to say this.

By the time I have left the desk, turned the page,
      you and your imaginary heart
will have moved to some other town, where perhaps,

you're lifting a fork or pulling the sheets again
      in a room full of windows.
I think of how small fires build a bed of hot cinders, how years

do nothing to sate my thirst for that corporal salt.
   How easy sex was then, back when my body
did not impede me.

Then it was all swift as gulls catching an updraft
   and winging it.
Once, I owned my lust. I did not stop.

Once, my whole body opened to desire,
   pushed you away,
even as I pulled you back in.

Prayer

What rewards the body / the body
a soldier / the body a name / a holiness

before sleep. Say you understood / say
nettles say feathers / say holy and mean

ancient / say homeward and mean gone
each shore-light falters / say my apologies

to your salt / oh lord / do not take yourself
to trial there are days / there are signs

in the dirt / whatever was meant
by the road is known only by the road

the mountain chase / the desert chase
the lake all rimmed in millweed

what child, what comes and should
I ask for the match / should I say please

days flame up like oil / please / I may beg
say that word / in my ear say it / so close

so I'll know whatever is given is received.

Transit

I know I'm supposed to look past the broken road
of morning, to not want to scoop the fog,
to put so much cloud in a cup.

Yet, here comes the ache heard
in the horsetail reeds at the passing of my car.

Beyond the ridge lined soldierly trees, the city,
the waning tracks and overpass bring us in.

I know I'm supposed to look past all the street's
narrow chances, shot through and shattering, the smashed

second story window while below the elderly open,
then move back into doorways marked for leaving.

Architecture overgrown, whiplash, plate of bones
left on the kitchen table, while last night's animal need
and hunt pack stay hidden.

Blue ligaments hold live oak's upended cement
and the dead street dogs soon to be lifted from their teeth.

Morning's little mutiny, petty-nothing-at-all,
but ritual of bowing to lantern of lover, to goodbye,
to marvel's opaque shadow and gristle of sunrise.

The hands set and set again to the bit shaft handle of work,
to the day's first graffiti in air I cannot read.

Birthday Poem

Whatever there is beyond
morning's scaffold

feels awful, just
awful today.

I want to say that going
on has its rewards, gives

a hope that ushers hope
and more, but of course

I am saying what is
is not enough,

ever, for any of us.

When you say this dark
is the arm of Christ's
forgiveness and his reminder

all I want is to clutch
at it, feverish as a lover

hasty, hard kissing
and fast, blundering

and pawing the someone
who is sure to walk in

and flip the lights
on all of it.

From First Lines by Marsden Hartley

Time and weather tear away
the houses that our fathers built

when they left them, and us in them
like ghosts of some unwanted season.

More the house than the idea,
more the flame of being

as we were brought into being
through flame, which is to say,

let me be clear—we were unwanted.
The world's a small place, really.

We keep running into each other.
I may remember something

that didn't happen; I may pray
before you as in a temple to who

I was with my hands tied
before me. Can I say that?

In school I sat as still as possible,
I did what I was told while the trees shook

with lightening and little flares.
The heart wanders the vacancies,

hides out and starts out again
through those woods confessing.

The heart tells the oldest story,
it calls a name, it finds a wound

like a house makes a perch in the night.

If I Have Wasted a Life

On its face the bed of small fires
flame up, messengers
from past regions
one never quite believed in.

As for ceremonies, there were plenty,
days arrived and passed each to each
as if clasped to a distant shoreline
that kept moving farther from sight.

Days of pleasures swallowing
pleasures swallowing sorrow.
Those dormant summers falling
into another unwanted season.

What was it that sighed inside you,
afternoons kicking up sand
and the little rag weed they called
Ambrosia or Common Aster?

Late October came as it always did
lit with ditch pyres and farmers
shouldering their tools
and heading home again.

Lengthening hours spent
doing nothing. Suppers
and then bathing, then bed.

But to be touched gently
on the shoulder by your mother's hand
at the end of it, with the horses
far off in the corner fields,

those great beauties grazing,
contented, their heads lowered
to the ceaseless task, their manes and tails
all smoky in the dusk.

Morning Among Strangers

The woman in the white walking hat leans
toward Orthodox Judaism. The other, older,
her hands in the bright air, says
her father the philanderer, dead
now for half a decade, is in hell.

Tipped on a tractor in the Middle West
and left until the helicopters came, the government
made them sift the dirt for contaminants
that cost the farm a thousand.
She says, I'm a libertarian down to my toes.

The family from Pottageville lost two
as infants, one to scarlet fever. Good thoughts, she says,
reminds me to pay my bills, to lick the hand
of the husband that feeds me. I'm grateful, you see,
for my children, savvy and thrift-driven, also, for the piper
who after these long days may show us all.

Ways of Sympathy

When I ask a man about his recent trip,
he says, look, there's value in experience, worth
in the act of moving through troubled lands.
These days it's all swift flights, easy taxi rides
to the beach. I shake my head. He says, what
we really need is a punishing bus ride
over rough terrain, long vistas, frosted peeks
high in the clean cold air where no one travels.
To be comfortably in pain is good and true
and purposeful. He tells me in Outer Mongolia,
for example, no one owns the land; it is a nation
of voyagers and the camps they stake are marked
by single smoke threads in the distance.
There's space enough for living and dying
alone. I saw long borders vanishing
off mapmaker's tables, entire ranges
left undefended, the greedy children we are
taught a lesson so elemental I felt in it
a secret pity. Beyond all the layers
of comfort and surfeit, even reason
and fear pull away. Hard to say this
to my friend who, going blind, childless,
who, having lost his mother said, yes, to science,
to scooping her sweet eyes and closing
the door on fire. Though I don't know, I do it anyway—
Say, look, beyond the ease of swift relief awaits
a brutal terrain and even farther
a coniferous Taiga where the biome
are mostly familial—arctic foxes, ermines,
wolverines at home in deep snow.

You flourish on a winter of sinew
and blood. You learn how to move again
among the boreal lichen, where pain and thrive
is the same faithful animal nature. I say, imagine…
your own fur, dense and remarkable
in the harsh winds.

Lines on Disaster

When the worst happens, as it does
like a proffer from the yawning
mouths of distant gods, I have already
thought of it. Not out of boredom
with astonishment but *in* astonishment
and always. Out in the yard deer have left
patent piles of scat again. My two-year-old daughter
lifts black pebbles to her mouth.
She's in her room now, punishing
her dolls, I know it. There are days the weight
of each distant disaster spreads full length.
Cholera like a grave ravaging the skeletal
bodies of the poor. A small animal
in a dark forest caught in a snare, gnawing
the bone. Those who are innocent
and those who are not. It does not matter.
Right now, eels are birthing their young
in the gaseous Sargasso Sea.
They are moving as usual toward the warm
slip-stream, and given the rising waters,
will be visible by morning.

Elegy for Carelessness

The little bird is caught
behind thin netting
made to hold fraying brick
from falling onto tourists
in the narrow lane.
Leaning into the breath
of the stone wall,
you watch its frenzied attempts
and willed release.
You see the sky
as only a slit-trench of light rushing.
You hear the low voices
moving away.
The things you have loved
are like that, ensnared
in something illusory
and looking back you see
that slim escape
you kept missing
in the mad flutter of days
that sets forth and
sets forth desire
and a terrible banging.

Whosoever Am I

In fields where most of the orchards are gone,
in wayward prairies wherever they are found
and in the split dark recesses

where land falls into itself, where
water seeps restlessly to its gathering.

Whosoever, but a sorrowing bone
turning sweet in the sun as if wind-fallen
from some bejeweled primal word

that tastes of sinew and packed
seed, claw and stone.

The orchard's secret on wing, on scat—
scattered mounds where none intrudes.
And when I say seed, I mean leeway,

that which travels, across waters, wanting
to be thrown shoreward in the wrack, I mean,

that which wrenches itself home.

The Falling

Beneath all of this is
a falling,
        which could only
be rain
in the evening, it…

could be
the sharp-toothed

in the flesh-made-whole, or a holiness,

        the choir all in robes.

How should I… I never knew
how anything worked,
                or cared.

Anyway, it's late. Too late to stop
a boy, half-piper, from walking
        into the sun tossing pennies
                over his shoulders.
They leap from the pavement
like ingots of flame
                where children follow.

Whoever He is, He has plans, tools of the trade,
your name
        is half-chiseled on his stone, you've
                always known it, the falling,
you feel it, like rain.

Porcelain Pictures in a Hilltop Cemetery, Spoleto, Italy

Under the nameless trees
the dead wear the faces of the living.
Their starched collars go on
being white. The way their smiles
outlive them and everyone
makes them feel like something for sale.

What is it? The man, Placido Aldimo
his oiled hair and a woolen coat
so tight no soul could squeak through.
Isn't a man's grave his final cage anyway?

If I could be with my dead I would do it here,
build a small house just big enough
for grief, a few lace curtains, fading
and flagrant in the sun.

Mostly the dead are old
and know they are dead.
Now the day keeper scratches
at the lane, carefully arranging
the smallest stones for the young.

My People

Upon setting foot on land, we would not be sated;
we wandered farther, following the sound of scythe
toward a flat camp called Lewis Bottom. But years before
we made it there was trouble in St. Louis, snow was falling
on the black brims of bowler hats in Chicago. They say
you'll know when the time to yield is right; we didn't.
The smoke-obscured century told a long wish
of sanctity and sin.

Always when our heels broke new dirt, the sound
was the same limp print saying westward.
The train tracks swelled like a grand suggestion,
a territorial history written in stitched labor.

We dragged our children behind us. We sold the horses.
Our women fell and were replaced. Each small town spoke
of angels and a god-awful outpost up ahead. We yearned for soil.
Our animal fur bristled in the wind.

In our country, there were bridges threading water,
windows floating through fields, houses, villages like a pack
of clapboard hounds huddled over a kill. And what began
as a slow journey blotched in sea-rime and no singing
from the boys in the hold, unfolded like a quilt of acres, dreaming
corn and sorghum. Each time we lit out as carefully packed freight,
it was the same rain that fell over new land.

In our bunks we dreamt of a common table, though the greatwheels
pounded out a terrible fury and the woodland darkness screeched
with migratory birds. They knew us from our moon-haunted

passage, from the low tones of the porter and the black speed,
from our steady iron-will to believe in anything that put us
in congress with the phantasmal ease of rushing over land.

To Pure Light and Sound

All winter I listen to his threadbare chords
through the firewall. The high and ghostly notes
rise above us and drift out over the Mississippi
which dozes under thin ice, and so hears
nothing. Boxcars coupling punctuate the night.
The old man never moves from the piano,
but for the one time, returning late, I caught him
stepping from the porch, circumspect and blind.

Later, he's in the kitchen in front of the old black and white,
which snows like the window above his bed, where,
come afternoon, he'll lie sleeping in a dream in which
he's awake again. He's at the piano. He's in the kitchen
testing the mayonnaise with a dim-nickeled knife.

This could be the dream of a man sleeping, or
the dream spreading around the man, becoming
the sheets that cover him in the shape of trampled snow
in a room without music.

Shadows rise slowly like carp surfacing
in the sun. He shrugs at nothing or himself
in the bathroom mirror and thinks
he is the unanswered question he keeps forgetting
to ask.

But tonight, under a blanket
of weak winter stars, he's Chopin again.
He's pure light and sound, the way a whistle
in a wet ally rises from the lips of a man walking
and whittles a little hole in the dark.

Overtime

I keep listening to the way the lake
spread out in black-caps and moon shimmer,

how that night the moon loved everything
it touched in black and white, turned the topsail

and rigging to silver in the bleak wind.
Silver coins, too, thick above us. We were still

young enough. Not lovers or lust driven, our friendship
road quietly on, neither of us saying much.

It would be the last trip across Gray's Bay, the end
of our last summer at home before we left

for different colleges. The long trains of loneliness
lay ahead, steaming in their yards, waiting,

though we could not have known it.
You were humming something by Neil Young, a Marlboro's

red eye singing the slow ash in your still boyish hand.
That night I did not deny or worry over

the coming shore. I lay back and let the tideless
reliable waters carry us, feeling fine

in your company, you, who had been kind
all of your life.

A Solitary Romance

Each day you dream the long story
of someone in love.
It is peace time.
You have books to read.
They pile on the table, the kitchen
floor. They lie exhausted as lovers
all over the bed.
The cat wants out. The coffee
burns in the pot. You have been busy
repairing the pages of sleep all your life.
Now you are tired. What you need is a rest
near the banks of the sacred stream.
Look, how beautiful the jeweled secret
of the speckled trout.
The page of the day is blank
and getting blanker. The spine is broken,
the words have flown.
What was it you meant to say
to a sky cross-hatched with wires
and its one moon, its transparent garment
hung only for you?
In the long avenues people are walking.
The dead walk past churches and synagogues.
The frozen river sleeps.
Then, without ceremony…there you are—
one of the inviolate survivors
of the corner shipwreck.
The flame is flickering. A storm is rising.
Somewhere black seeds hidden in black soil
are taking root.

Your House by the Sea

—after "Zoning," a painting by Matt Brown

Imagine spending year after year
in a town where no one notices
the common grace of a Crepe Myrtle
in the park or the boon of any living thing
so they cease to appear. The one
escape is a country of paint.

You pack your bags and go there.
It's easy; each day a horizon
without history, inside it—
vetch and heather, the deadpan sea
outside your door.

What has happened and is happening
is up to you. Nothing can move until
you find the word. You say, *yarrow*
and it's tumbling across the dunes.
You say, *house*—it rises before you.

Days you listen to nothing, and the perfect song
of nothing. You grow to love and hate
the stillness of the frame. But come evening
the moth on the wooden table spins itself
into myth, until you say *stop.*

Then one day the sky opens to that one bird
that stands for South or beauty, or brevity;
only longing was meant to last. Poor bird,
poor North one has to return to
and not know why.

Far off, a man in shirtsleeves is struggling
a wheelbarrow up a hill. Now your old neighbor
hangs limp clothes on a line and the whole world
goes damp. What does it matter?

Above this sea the sky holds and holds its rain.
And that hum, as if your own mother was here—
her voice, that one syllable, say it, *love.*

The Future of Anywhere

It could be winter again in 1916, Jack London,
in his death dream, is still sailing to Tahiti

and the gristmills of the east are starting up.
The dogs gather into troops to tear the meat

from the meat. There may be pirates
along any coast. Fires burn endlessly.

There will be collapse and surge of armies
clashing where no one sees. Before this it was

always wars and death and birth
and perhaps a bit of the bird in the breast

of a few. What's changed? Outside the window
the cold wind still pushes its way and wins.

Not even in Stockholm or Minsk are they
used to this. The good gentleman warm

their barrel chairs in the club where the golden
whiskey cannot melt ice. April, May, then

June again with sweet violet. Some woman's
hair scented to swoon. The soldier hears moonlight

pooling by his cot; the mind of the child
holds the wings of moths, and the wind again

rises in the open field, stirring its comrades, while
the future opens its curtain to this and this and this.

Faint Singing

There are times the morning
is the good day blossoming,

a kindness that opens simply
because it must.

Even in distance, we find it
and then that muscular pain of habits

and fears is released or all at once
understood. But the day's poverty

may just as likely be silence, that sun
a landmine of becoming, or stories

of a frigid dawn before singing. Whatever—
a murmur of arguments, insidious mandrakes

one never quite believes in. *He went out*, she said,
he went out and never came back.

The idea was of a world and so much pain,
also, the quiet tickings of the house

set against it. So much stillness to be taken in.
The terrible news, the car engine catches

and roars, hours pass, men and women lean
at lunch tables, whisper *darling, darling,* desiring

it so, and so it helps a little—entering a blank day
feeling for the precious silk, an intimacy,

kept pressed and buried, unused even,
in your mother's dark drawer.

Love & Arthur Ashe, 2005 North America

What was it the old American standing
in El Jardin, San Miguel, Mexico
said of La Cucaracha? *I'm rich; this is my dog,*
and this one here…You have old eyes.
Do you have a smoke? His paintings
he said, were mural-sized homages
hung in some hillside grotto
over-looking the sculpted trees
of the park, the domes and spires rising
through the perpetually pink sunscapes,
beyond which the land dipped
to dry plains and an occasional cactus
stuck on a rise like a joke.
The night was warm and scented
with cigar smoke. Weeks passed
in the immaculate white-washed
apartment of guitar music, where lazily
we made love, drank our wine
from juice glasses and read all
the *New Yorkers* left there.
Sometimes you on the bed, me
in the other room closest the open
doors of the balcony where below
the prehistoric and prehensile
creatures lumbered clumsily
under the lamps. It was love
as it happens, past urgency
an almost solitary comfort.
What was it that one was saying?
Oh yes, Clarence was in the square,
among trees and people, talking Kerouac
and Cassady and his childhood friend,
that famous tennis player

from Richmond, dead of Aids
now for decades. He was talking.
He was richer than all of us
and we walked with him
to the oldest bar
where he left the dog outside
and we went in like kings, like
indigents, and bummed cigarettes
off of the dead.

The Gossip of the Bins

Look at you sitting there, huddled close,
your yawing mouths tied quiet now.
What slept inside you all night unbothered
by claw or feral snout? A body so obviously alive
with rot must be a happy container for the dead.

What carnival? What riotous silence beyond our hearing
has nothing to say to the living? The flesh that has stepped
out of the flesh, reduced to refuse, only what is left.

And was I right to sleep unaware, my window open, to rise
and walk as if my hunger is never abated?
A body needs and needs. And what is left is too much.
The day warms; the beautiful runners pass
in the street, their brown bodies clean with sweat
while beside me, here, screaming their angel-winged
hearts, red begonias drop multitudes of blossoms.

The City America

The dog tied outside the bar is uninterested
in Philadelphia or Fargo, or any place bereft

of the doggie life. Across the street a motel pool
is filling, while down at the pier the boys are hopping

the gates with their legends and beach ball buoys,
hoping for the lost mines of the Pacific or Atlantic.

What does it matter? The equatorial evening is only a dream
with a filched watch, waiting to beat some child

left in a park. Where to find all that was worshipped
and lost, how to wake at dusk to the gifts a hole leaves,

a desire, or a cruelty that seethes and snags on the places

we inhabit? Wherever the body forgets it is soft
is sadder than finches, more in need of humility

than the kid whose only harbinger
is the poem of hope tattooed on his back,

stolen even, and too remote to read.

Tremolo

A few moments before the first throb
in the evening air, the frogs begin
out in the muck-slung swamp
beyond the low fence. An unhurried chorus
tries the woodwinds, then the high strings
of desire. It fills the spaces between
cypress knees, slash, and long-leaf pine.

The storm is a swift waterfall of hail
drumming, then a sudden spreading stillness
that breaks into a wild frog-happy racket again.

To be amphibious and without time,
to make the whole forest alight with pleasure,
yearning, half-falling off logs and rough trunks,
an open and closed call, the song, the long low
blow of sex sex sex.

Everywhere the good life is calling us home.
It becomes possible, again, to be young and in love,
to call to those that would have us, and those
beyond our having. The heavy industry
of pungent disorder, an arable house of life.
The gravel and pitch of jubilance that says—
This is the time. This is the place.

The Secret

The opossum's meandering tracks
and mud mounds are his morning love-note

and I the mistress to his crepuscular
visitations. Shaggy hide and pointed snout,

pink rimmed with raw baldness.
Stiff whiskers brush up offal and leaf, the delicacy

of kitten kibble I've left on the back porch.
The opossum bumbles the steps, a clumsy

prideless guest with unembarrassed rat tail,
which he drags behind him. Poor rough creature,

rain-soaked and nearly blind. You could be
tame as a dog thrown from a passing car.

You make your home wherever you go
and do not, though often believed,

hang from the slim branches of trees
by your tail. Though, you carry your babies,

all of them, on your aching arched back
and feed them from each sweet teat

and sometimes you can be seen openly,
thrown sideways with your maw wide

to the road, lit for a moment by my car
lights, showing us all your rows of prehistoric

vicious teeth, exposed like a warning
of what you could have, but almost never, used.

We Thought We Heard Rain

We didn't know what woke us, just
a kind of drop and swirl.
The state had been bound in drought
all summer and in the dark
deer moved though the yard
taking the second blush
of the youngest rose.
They pulled the heads
from the velvet-throated petunia
in the flower box, but left a long
bitter leg of it, broken.
By morning the ringed-neck doves
returned, hunting the pine-straw
with their woody hollows
and dry pronouncement.

The day before, I had stood smoothing
my grandmother's credenza
with the lemon-wet of a flannel cloth.
I breathed, but moved carelessly, while
the lawn grayed in heat and a shift
of starlings wavered a pool of dust.
I watched them form from the window
a disappearance that hung persistent
above and below until
I remembered the undeniable, how
the little arrows point away from the good
animal heart until one gives up
or in, as if the living was a great stretched
and burdened sinew. One hears some wild
unexpected congregation and goes out into it.

I took up the hose, held it high
like a mercy to cool them in the mist
from the parallel globes arching and gleaming
where the satiate fell.
But only I felt a brief benevolence,
some infinite pleasure glistening
on the shoulders of this world.

The starlings, perceiving only a temporary
breaking and the simple unlikelihood
of kindness, startled up in dark armament,
in a gesture of receding rain. And in one swift breath
made for the high dead branches of the elm.

Child at Zoo

Her double reflects when pressed to the penguin exhibit
with its unfrenzied stasis, its long tank set in a window

made to look cool as low mountains. The water moves
without sound to the bird's bob or sway in its tideless current.

On the phony ice, some stand or walk under the dim electric sun.
It is not a deep plunge the small one takes. Does he glimpse

the child's eye, the meditator of the long deathless sleep,
or does he see her floating there as a dark shadow

of some foreign vegetation, fish shaped,
in the deepest sea at dawn?

Lock Down Drill Day

Sweet rot of tea olives dusty with autumn
in the school yard. Past mock red octagon

and two crossings of cracked sidewalk capering
when here they come. Whatever they are at home, here

they are children in uniforms, late afternoon, hot shoes
huffing up sand past raised garden boxes

of big-eared kale and snapdragon's pallid maw.
Behind iron gates, the stone fish pond buoys

lily pad-clogged and ardent with moss undulating.
A flag hangs still, flagrant, and buzzing.

My daughter carries her class project
cautiously, confident as a baker

with a wedding cake on a platter.
All night we worked the miniature diorama

of her bedroom—brightly woven rug, wooden dresser,
two minute whip-stitched bedside lamps,

and grandmother's love-quilted roses
covering the imperative yarn-made doll of herself

who, each day, comes home to her bed dreaming.

Our Time

With the day's distractions softened to blue shadow
up in her room, she whispers her eight-year-old sadness,
her secret guilt, the covert unkindnesses, the time

she claimed her classmate with Down's slapped her face.
She says, sometimes she really did hit me, bit me, but not
the time I told. My daughter trusts our secret pact, which

stipulates my silence. I do what I can, I rub her back
until her voice in the dark is all she from me pouring
forth again. She fills and fills until we spill into
the common cup of our listening.

Without advice or reproval, I swallow her whole day
that feels like dull pencils, worn paper, and the hopelessness
of each eraser doing its poor work of hiding the mistakes.

The Host

I had no idea that waking at 3a.m. to enter fully
my worry, would be a welcome to the day,

almost every day the same street on which
the still house continues, the glasses being washed

by hand and set to dry on a striped towel beside
the sink so clean. This is what you do, I think,

hitting my hand on the metal chair left pulled out
at the café, someone, a man, leaving things in disarray

wherever I go. It does no good to know
the photographs you framed hang in some

beautiful house in St. Paul. You're gone into a winter
forever. This is how to laugh, you used to say to me.

And I'd say, how? Like this? Like this you'd say,
wandering down the unlit part of the long hall.

A Harvest

First the rains came hard and long
and loved the open field envious
of blackbirds. Everyone kept
their distance, except for lovers
for whom her skin shown
like a skein of light.

And when the survivor of storms
could be felt in the muscle's need
to stretch, the whole body swelled,
darkened her sex, her desire
so like a pitiless need
to mark out new territories,
to make use of tools, ancient and divining
the directions, a string of feathers
and nettles strung on the fence.

In the end there was no choice
but to open to the chancellor of other.
Mother or child, which living root
of the animal was set to fire?

Concerning the Axe

What Snyder says is true—
when making the handle of the axe
by cutting wood with an axe, the model is indeed
close at hand. If it weren't, why would so many
young among us, after the high seat of adult cruelty
presents itself, learn how to cut the air
with sharp-edged bodies, the precision
of their instrument always cocked
for any opportunity. But especially
for the child, the woman
with child, the animal with the wide
open heart of a field, they seek to plow
to put to good use, a use, for the tool
they've carefully crafted and been
crafted by, the art of tacit mimicry.

Annunciation

In the waiting room, or at the party,
or even in the park on an afternoon

with the sun warming the palm fronds
to glitter, and the curious peripatetic

squirrels moving unmolested, anywhere
a new mother of one or two daughters

will hear how not hitting, not shoving,
not the energy-ball-of-boy, but an early blossoming

innate bitchiness is sure to be her child's lot.
It's not a joke. They'll say it to the moon face

of the child herself, who sits carefully arranging stones,
gathering in the hard expectations of her soul's

true nature. She won't move or look up
to what alights, which is to say is preordained

as one woman to another. As if
the child learning early the art of stillness

is grace, not a smooth retaliation
but a matter of manners. She is learning

the thin-lipped smile, the looking away,
the same slim escape her mother feels

gathering her child's full human weight, gathering
in the supplicant nature of all the Marys

who kneel, doing what little there is
before giving her child over to the world.

Girls Riding Lesson

When I see my daughter swing up
to straddle the horse, I lean back
against the fence to watch. Heat prickles
the spike-weed at my bare ankles.
The other girls are not much younger
or older. Gallons of water stills
the trough filled to almost spilling.
They begin in two-point, heels down
toes up in the stirrups, moving
in circles, in the dirt cut path
and tufted grass the ring makes.
They will heed the lessons of the woman
on the ground, the one yelling out
encouragement and correction.
They will keep their eyes to their own
horse's ear tips as if in
great concentration, as if
there is a truth they are seeking
that is real as air, the body's
burgeoning awareness, which is not
casual to the world.
Already they know it. All around
the news is bad. They may be seen,
but not heard, they may be taken
against their will. There is danger
outside the barracks. Whatever
connections they have made
of the old story of predator
and prey, they keep to themselves.
Their faces are set fierce
against the lees of fate.

They hold their bodies taught
to the mass of muscle moving
beneath them. They hold tight the reigns
against what might without warning,
turn against them.

Any Given Night

Isn't it something to know how in sleep
the day's big reveries concede
to the yard's emergent calm?

Scent of spice rising and the neighbors
gone so quiet. The owl's minor notes
through lowland swamp casts its hollow sorrow

over our rooftops. All night I seem to sleep
among branches, pale shadows forgiving
as starlight. All night I rest godlike in my senses

until I am numinously aware of some small forager
tearing grass outside my window, chewing methodically,
divinely remote in its animal pleasure.

Foreign City

The moment the rain diminished in the streets
       I began to love the rain. This is always the case.
What I have loved is the way each thing held close to the body
       becomes filament
                  until it no longer exists.

And if the damp wood-must rose in the cathedral
       for any unholy reason, I don't want to know.
The gothic spires gestured toward God.

When the light shifted in evening,
       what did the black Vltava remember
of the rain? The swans had become a dull gray with it
       and swam into a kind of disappearing and undisappearing.

Rain no longer in the lamp light's angle, in fact
       no longer falling at all
above the giant horse chestnuts in the park
       that slept and went on sleeping and caring
 for no one.

Overlooking it all I can see my loneliness
       was perfect,
and I gave it a name; itinerant, harbinger, ash.

Take now, the familiar music heard for a moment
       through an open window of a taxi, or
the woman in blue who stared so hard
       out of the painting I had to go back
to look again. Behind all of her intention

I recognized a man I had loved, and whose love for me
        grew vagrant.
Once, while walking in Hradcany Gardens
we stepped off the path to rest.
        He had laid his head on my lap and slept.
Stilled, his face looked troubled in sunlight
        as if a countenance could contain cloud-drift
and hint at a fear of water.
He must have formed a different city
        in his sleep.
Little by little twin creases in his brows
        seemed to suggest plowed fields

and a ditch filling with rainwater.

In that moment what became small
        was the simple expression of affection, the head
listing to one side, the hand of the man loosening
        into its own dream, beyond the tiered garden
in which the sparrow, nesting in the perfect idea of trees
        becomes what it always meant to become—
a songbird whose song you hear

this moment and not that one,
        its staccatos and spondees
rises and drifts above you
        until persuaded by nothing at all
it descends again like the head of a lover
        into the pale upturned landscape
of your palms.

Ode to a View Through a Window with Fear of an Elegy Inside It

What do I know of birds, numberless as they are?

Not the few pipers like emissaries there, but that
every bird I see is yours, your blackbird heart, superstitious,
back in the Midwest, hearing voices.

Yesterday, I was sure your breastbone breached
in the lilt of your throat.

Now the boats in the bay all careen to the west.
The sun is out from under the cold hood of its moon

and all the people walking in the street below
seem to be calling to someone.

Wherever I travel, whichever window I look through,
there you are, holding out some dark hatchling,
offering a worrisome old life for the new.

Aubade

In the name of beginnings
the morning smells like horseshit
and coffee. At the open market
stout men and women
move with ease, question
after which vegetable, is the fruit face
blushing enough?

The terrible opera singers rush
through the square in garish
hats. Their large voices push
the air around like dump trucks
blackening an ally.

I feel sloppy
and wash my mouth of its bitterness
but the darkness returns.

There are several small dogs
on the avenue today, glancing
sidelong at one another.

Landscape with First Line by Norman Dubie

The birches stand in their beggar's row.
Each field is brief and cordoned off
by shrubs, and somewhere a wild boar
raises its snout to a northern wind.

Across the broken roof tops sunlight reaches
to where two men stand, turning sand
to mortar. It is the oldest sound—water
poured one vessel to another.

This is the way you reach a country
cleansed of your defiance—you must build
and rebuild from the unearthed upward.
The archeology of the heart creaks
in its harness.

The men have stopped now, are standing
in smoke. Whatever is hidden
stays hidden. Whatever is filling,
fills like a grave.

A Mexican Vision

Behind the Iglecia de las Mañanas, Maximillian's walled gardens
open again to Birds of Paradise, squat palmettos, and the courtyard
rimmed in flagstone, beyond which twin rowboats are moving over

the pond's unbreakable surface. If you agree to the secret door
his lover used in the nineteenth century, you may be allowed
to enter without diversions of the heart. Your cotton skirts catch

on the branches that want nothing to do with wealth. Sunlight
on a bare thigh. You are not married. You have no parents.
The new German priest arrives and settles his hands in the water

table by the window. You fear all the Indians of the world
are dead, but for the birds they worshipped, embroidered
all over the white breast of your blouse.

By Night, by Rail

West reports tunnel, reports darkness,
East, thresholds, windows—
cut outs—cherry warm.
My body, so good at moving,
goes where I cannot. So good,
at looking, as if someone else,
doing things only someone else
would do. Here folds the napkin
into fourths, covers lips, two rings
on my hands or a different woman's
standing at a sink in memory?
We, both of us, are less and less
until wholly discarnate.
In the valley, a darkness
does not care.
And who knows what lies
beyond the windows'
little disturbances.
Chopin's head, severed
after death, was lost, though
his heart, they said, spirited
to Holy Cross church
by night, by rail.

How Little it Matters

Say boats crowd a pier / the small docks heaving with rigging /
a man singing something foreign and smooth / as morning water
on a shallow bay. / Say it is leaving time, and say it without cost.
The room you kept you leave / you leave unmade, / a light /
a little music playing / the radio / on the shelf. Say it is all it takes
for longing, the room emptying. / Say without you, / it sounds,
from this distance, as if a satisfied crowd is rising / to welcome all
the windows home.

Two Views of Loss

I.

A river rises with heavy rains and can't imagine where the swell
comes from. Its choppy overflow resembles the cobbles beyond
the hand-built blockade of slumped sand-filled sacks. Its waters
are happy in the defeated lands.

II.

The common swallow, whose nest is expertly crafted under
the rigid girders of the bridge, refuses to leave. Each spring
is another bad season for the hard-won hatchlings lost
to the mud-bubbled shores below.

The Trouble with My Version of Events

The weather man says, *all calm,* but when I look again
the sea is at the stairs. Everything stained yellow,

also, rain.

Three miles of granite causeway
draws in the silvering fish. Someone places
a dollar in my mouth, asks, are you getting this?

Each step is treacherous, though the ground stones
feel solid.

What is left on either side is not.

I know the rules, the farther out, the funnier
the trick of sea and sky, that's why the jetty

exists. The moment I turn for home, here comes
the flood. I can't feel it, but I fear a turbulence

underneath. The more water washes them away,
the more I fear the buoyancy of my feet.

Farthest Point Out

Sails like spindrift, cloud scud, skipjack fields, / the day full of
sleepers, the summer almost, almost… North most / on a switch of
beach / to the last horizon. I throw my lines / underbelly broke by
sea, by what / fixes me sky-pinned. Blue ether. / So many of them,
each disturbance / in air / a thin ladder to sky.

For a Friend Going Blind

I close my eyes to see the shape
the rain makes of the tin-roofed porches
and the spouting drain's serpent
of smooth motion.

Whatever judgement in the near trees
is drowned.

There is a light to sound, but
I'm no good at this.

I have no picture or memory
that cannot be corrupted
or given rise by a new light.

Hearing the sea in the evening traffic
sings back the great wildness, the trick
of not seeing the whole dark wonder of it,
as I feel for the edges of its falling
that does not fall.

The Primary Divide

As if a man alone in a theatre
on a summer afternoon.
The film, yet to begin
in the trice indeterminate dark.

That sparking overhead,
only false star-glitter
of pantomime distraction.

While the block make-up
of the fabrication
castle walls insinuate
encroaching shade.

The vanishing, a madness
of Achilles, the queries
of a royal betrayed
and betrayed as one aspiring
not to godhood, not desiring
more than what once was,

but the enduring filament
of a single note that says,
the real god of memory
is the primary divide,
that first light a storybook,

and then the angel
in autumn leaves, the way
water ignites a wash
barely green, nightly equations
of windows and the disbelief
of the harlequin shadow
on the bedroom floor.

It seems real, like the little
flaring of a match
in the center of the screen
after the TV went dark, a haunting
you could not touch or hear.

What the Man Said

—For D.M.

But there is always a horse race
      somewhere in the world.
And wherever there is one, there is also
      a wall of televisions
all tuned to a different track and the tracks go on
      in a multitude
of heats for much of the day, really, no matter
      what day it is, and if you bet enough
they'll give you drink tickets
      at the window
so you will stay and bet some more.
      That's what it's all about, the sure thing
or the impossible odd
      and doing it no matter what
the bank, your wife, or anyone says,
      you're here and you are here
to lay down your silver on something
      and if you don't understand this
you will never understand anything.

A Student in Poetry Is Writing a Poem

A student in Poetry I is writing a poem
about hitting a mule deer with his truck
over winter break in Wisconsin.
He begins with the evening road, which hid a scrim
of salt ice and the trees at the road's edge
he says, darkened and rose up in nervous effigy.
The deer, smallish, young, suddenly there
breaking the blue trance of horizon.
He writes the poem and thinks the words
colliding on the frozen landscape of the page
are all wrong. No good. No help at all.
He reads the poem out loud to the class
and thinks there is no way to say how
the sound, even inside the closed cabin
of his hearing was all at once brittle
as heavy sticks perfect for fire, broken dry
over his knee when he was younger
and still in love with fire. How it was also
yielding and easy as flecked fur slipping under
the light touch of a child's hand.
He reads the poem and looks small
and cold in a t-shirt faded thin, illegible.
To simply insist the heart understand
a sorrow that splits and gives way
and disappears finally, where it would be easy
to end, perhaps, before the tenderness
undresses on the page like it always does—
criminally wild and shamefully scant.
Who doesn't want the path through
the heavy woods never to cease,
where one cannot see too far ahead?

Precision

Straight off the brush the sticky pigment
of Indian Bone, Moroccan-Wash, or
White-Earth covers the smudge
of scuff in the halls where students
turn into classrooms unaware
of the long arm of the young sweeper
who moves methodically, his pockets
full of tabby. Each day the packs,
the papers, the scritch of seats
ache with the weight of what might
be fortune. Still, there are the ones
who cover the unsightly, sweep the leftovers,
the empties from corner bins, the dance
of the cleaners, the soap fillers, the painters,
the painters whose strong arms know
the practice of precision, who carry
their buckets two, four at a time
skillfully down packed stairways past
psychology, biology, and mathematics.
In muted shirts sweat-stained
and smelling of good salt, the muscle's
need to stretch is clear and the words
of the fortunate blow over their heads
like notes set to strokes north and south.
They stoop to the good work done
the with the care of town's keepers
oiling the gates, beyond which the dogs
of mediocrity are kept, so that the children
of the careful, the quick, the beloved,
might easily pass through.

Impulse Control

The study suggests that if a child fails
to refuse marshmallows, petite as baby-teeth,
offered on a white plate, impulse control
will be a problem all of his life.
The TV spokesman in a dark suit points—
Here we have the overeater, the drinker, the hoarder.
But if the child learns early, say
before the age of eight, that
more marshmallows will arrive
if he sits and waits, a good dog,
then will-power will be set
and the talent for avoiding trouble
for himself or others will benefit
us all. What should be done?
I imagine sudden colonies of puptents
arriving in towns like traveling
revivals, the sweet voices of the ones
who provide. The ones who hold the keys
to a reward always to come later
if only we believe now. And what fortunes?
Money, happiness, the ridiculous jest
of perfect love? The world may tip
with all we've been promised—
Even the world to come, a prescribed beauty
not our own. The small men and women seen
from above and the great benefactor
in the clouds, sensing our tension as we
walk to school, to work, to the overly
greenly-lit grocery store. What thoughts or
returns or wool-making for a small child
sitting at a table, being told—take, eat,
this is the good body of the world
you must learn to live without?

The Way with Students

We're sitting around the circle
like we do and I am being the me
they know and the me they don't.
Most days I live in terror of saying anything
that rises above my meaning.
Inside the room there is another sky
and sometimes it appears
unbroken, but the truth is it *is*
broken, even though I want us all
under it together, indivisible, caught
on this side of presage, like a light falling
all of a kind. Someone desires leaves
through a bedroom window, someone
feels the bush for a switch, someone else
grabs a knife. There are whole days
moving out of the valley toward a wide slope
where anything might happen.
When I come home, the roses I never liked
have grown leggy and wild. My daughter
runs and whoops in green circles singing.
And the feral cat, usually so elusive, moves
through the boxwoods, lifting her face to me,
her body a shapely code, her voice barely there.

The Greatest Trick

The women are bound lip to lip
as if kissing could save them.
That strip of morning light crossing
over the rocks along the Hudson.
And the men who find them ask, *How
could this happen?* As if the world
is not the world we made. All my life
I have seen rivers, Mississippi
from the high bridge and frozen bluffs
of St.Paul where mornings mushroomed
up, then faded into ordinary day.
Women disappearing into shadows
and cloaks, that is, until
the moment the light finds them,
buys them, sells them for all to see.
The newsman turned barker
at the carnival of our despair.
Women disappear and reappear,
a magic trick for the darkness we call
the madness of Greek necessity. We
fall in love with our loss; we say paradise
has costs we must bear. We say
how beautiful they are, bound by breast
and hip. Look, the lips are touching
softly still.

Sleeping with Jesus

Fearing death would have her if He
was not bound and pressed under

the clean sheets of her pillow,
my college roommate, the only

one I would ever have, went to bed
daylight early, believing the devil's whispers

might find her in the dark vacuum
of our tiny shared room.

Everywhere she walked, she saw it—
Devil on her dinner plate, godless death

waiting in the subarctic blast
that blew through the Upper Midwest.

I listened to her breath at times
become a mantle or veil to vaper.

As if from the heights of a pulpit
she rose, a clergy of one.

Though I saw her hesitate once
in a hallway to witness two girls

on their knees, facing east
in this hemisphere of benediction.

No stone between us, no words
a friction of discord, but she knew

my secret history of doubt.
No doubt I woke her, sneaking

in late with a candle set to read
something borrowed.

How could she know what drew me
into the emptied chapel blue afternoons

cloaked in my cargo of loneliness.
The nuns moved soundlessly and did not

come near. The older ones, no doubt,
intimately familiar with wounds and failures,

all the radiant distractions of prayer,
that terrible cold collateral.

Strawberries

I'd never known such fruit before
I stole it. O, how they take on earth and
turn white blossom's yellow heart to sweet.
How to trust a thing eternal as my hunger,
a root or dark pendulum balancing where
desire bridges the days. And should I be
grateful to forget what pleasures I've taken
to tongue? Must I pocket the pretty blade
atop the plump soft heft in the hand?

Court Ship

That year I didn't know the stones
you offered were ballast; nor

could I imagine another shore
among the friable lichen

and granite crops where you slept
free of worry. It had little to do

with me. Lone gunman with joke
weapons, a storehouse cave for the loot,

some desire for sex that seemed
beyond mere wanting. You were collecting

a whole for the parts—worker, mother,
house-cleaner, wife. Your work was all

stripping to put to use, to have,
to simply have and to hold.

In Praise of Feminism

In 1974, the women of Fairfax Elementary Library
were still librarians. Still Mrs. or Miss, their pastel twin-sets
held at the throat by delicate chains ornamented
with tiny paste jewels, or their cat eyes hung there
on their breasts by lanyards made of small imitation pearls.
The sound of stockings was a soft hush-hush,
as powdery as the perfume that clouded over us as we sat,
twenty third graders on the floor where we were so used
to sitting, close enough to inspect the indiscriminate wear
of each navy Maryjane and red Ked, close enough again
to the familiar child scent of urine and sleep.
I hardly knew anything then and wasn't about to learn.
So interested was I in the dream of the tree moving
in a hot autumn wind outside the window
where small sparrows darted freely through the branches.
Back then, the librarian's bleached hair
was still a thing called *frosted* and I stared
at her cloud of teased and sprayed bouffant,
at her pink perfection fingertips, her dainty
sugared lips, her icicle blue eyelids with envy.
I don't recall ever using the Dewey Decimal System
of the card catalog she taught us, so long defunct, as she,
by now, must also be. I prefer to think she didn't care
if we didn't learn, that she cherished us all the same
in her safety and fulfillment—smiling, happy
in her marriage, her own mother's white gold watch ticking
out an extinction, braceleted like love to her slim wrist.

Snow Season

Snow was the seduction of a white gown
that built in twilight-mass our desire for more.

It sway-backed the powerlines, though
it was only a kind of progress, we understood.

Of course, there were the starving months
I marched into, called it love or safety.

Like sugar for salt or blade for the tongue,
I pulled the sheets until the bed

bent or broke at the slats. I leaned
into that hunger willingly.

How to choose despair by degrees?
Can I say, honestly, I chose my body?

How could I know fear, also, packed in
a life-debt of loneliness like ice crystals,

cold, blank, and only the start of a new year?

These Things Happen

—For Jim Moore

It is the saying of parents and grandparents,
an old explanation meant to soothe
one new to this world who sits in teary
bewildered aftermath
of an accident or unexplained cruelty.
I grew up hearing it this way: *these things happen*
says the coach to the child at the park
who swung the unwieldy bat
right into the catcher's face.
These things happen soothes the mother
to her heartbroken daughter, her
sorrowful son. It's our way of saying
we understand, get used to expecting
the unexpected, the heart's a tender place after all,
and the world at times merciless for no reason.
A squirrel races across the tree-lined street
then changes direction right
before my car's heavy tires.
Somewhere a tractor tips in a far-field.
The days are marked
by what we can control
and what we cannot. A woman travels
through dark snow-laden streets.
She is listening to the song on the radio
play out a sadness she knows is truer
than true. A father loves his daughter
but never tells her. A child is sent to bed early
on the night of the terrible storm.
We sit in pews longing for answers.

We ask the air, our eyes moving from the hymnal
to the window and back again. These things happen,
reminded my good friend when I couldn't speak
for all the reasons of the world, sitting in the freezing café
and crying into my coffee.

More than Dreamtime

The bird that has died overhead sings a song.
—James Dickey

Cielo, sky, there it is lo mismo. I am bi-lingual
of small migratory genus, I go on thinking

I am part of it. The avalanche of sun bears
in my slumber. Cat wakes, uncurls in flower pot

below. I go on thinking about daylight
about birds torching the air by wing. I stare

still skyward, abajo abajo the code breaker
the garden clouds, atras, I may be reborn.

Nuthatch and redbird staccato, yes, cardinal.
Cicada screech Que intiende? I am a failed species,

all finished and baked on dark metal roof for months,
my mouth an open pike to thunderstorms.

My grease-smear stuck, inteligencia, the lawn.
Well, then, I am dead and the day is not.

Blowing Smoke

I had wanted to keep the fires,
my bed made low by blowing
embers and so be lifted
into starlessness.

I had wanted to wash in shocking
river water, but something said, *No,
there are limits.* Who makes the laws
that live within the thatched rent grasses
of a breast? I set out to caves, towards

mud-packed cliffs, frozen temperatures
at dawn among creatures made
of necessary armor, claws sheathed
and unsheathed in their joints.

When I arrived, all domesticity
lived within the hours, a confinement,
the ground waters gone, and my garden—
a wild calling across years.

About the Author

A.M. Brandt received her MFA from the University of Minnesota. She has been an Edelstein Keller, Presidential, and Gessell Writers Fellow, as well as a Lexi Rudnitsky Prize semi-finalist. Her work in *Parhelion Literary Magazine* has been nominated for Best of the Net, and she has been an AWP Intro Journal Award and Ruth Lilly Poetry Contest Finalist. A.M. teaches literature and writing at Savannah College of Art and Design in Savannah, Georgia, where she lives with her husband and daughter.

www.ingramcontent.com/pod-product-compliance
Lightning Source LLC
Chambersburg PA
CBHW022013080426
42733CB00007B/586